WE
BUILD
OUR
HOMES

For Zachary, just like I promised.
L.K.

For Elliot, Nora & Olive.
C.M.

Quarto is the authority on a wide range of topics.
Quarto educates, entertains and enriches the lives of
our readers—enthusiasts and lovers of hands-on living.
www.quartoknows.com

© 2018 Quarto Publishing plc

Laura Knowles has asserted her right to be identified as the author of this work.
Chris Madden has asserted his right to be identified as the illustrator of this work.

Art Director: Susi Martin
Creative Director: Malena Stojic
Publisher: Maxime Boucknooghe

First published in 2018 by words & pictures,
an imprint of The Quarto Group.
6 Orchard Road
Suite 100
Lake Forest, CA 92630
T: +1 949 380 7510
F: +1 949 380 7575
www.QuartoKnows.com

A CIP record for this book is available from the Library of Congress.

ISBN 978-1-910277-82-9

Manufactured in Dongguan, China TL062018

9 8 7 6 5 4 3 2 1

MIX
Paper from
responsible sources
FSC® C104723

WE BUILD OUR HOMES

Words by Laura Knowles
Pictures by Chris Madden

words & pictures

Contents

Born to Build

What are the best things about having a home?

Our homes are places we share with our families.

Our homes are places where we can feel warm and comfortable; where we can rest and feel safe.

Animals build for the same reasons. Many build nests where they can raise their babies in safety, away from predators.

Others build homes where they can stay warm through the winter, or cool during the hot summer months.

Some creatures build a place where they can store their food. There are even a few who build simply to impress a mate.

While we build homes that last for many years, many animals must build a new home every year. Their survival depends on it.

Each story in this book is true. They are stories of incredible animal architects; animals that, just like us, were born to build.

We are the **Tailorbirds**.

The needle-beaked nesters.

The female is the one who builds, while the male keeps guard. We don't want any other tailorbirds stealing our spot!

To make the nest, we poke holes along the edge of a large leaf.

Next we sew it together to make a cone. Now, what in a forest would make a good sewing thread...?

We choose spiderweb or plant fibers.

Inside the leaf, we weave
a delicate cup of grass,
softened with cotton,
feathers, and fur.

We lay our precious eggs.

We are so careful with
our sewing that the
leaf stays alive and
green—the perfect
camouflage to
keep our chicks
hidden.

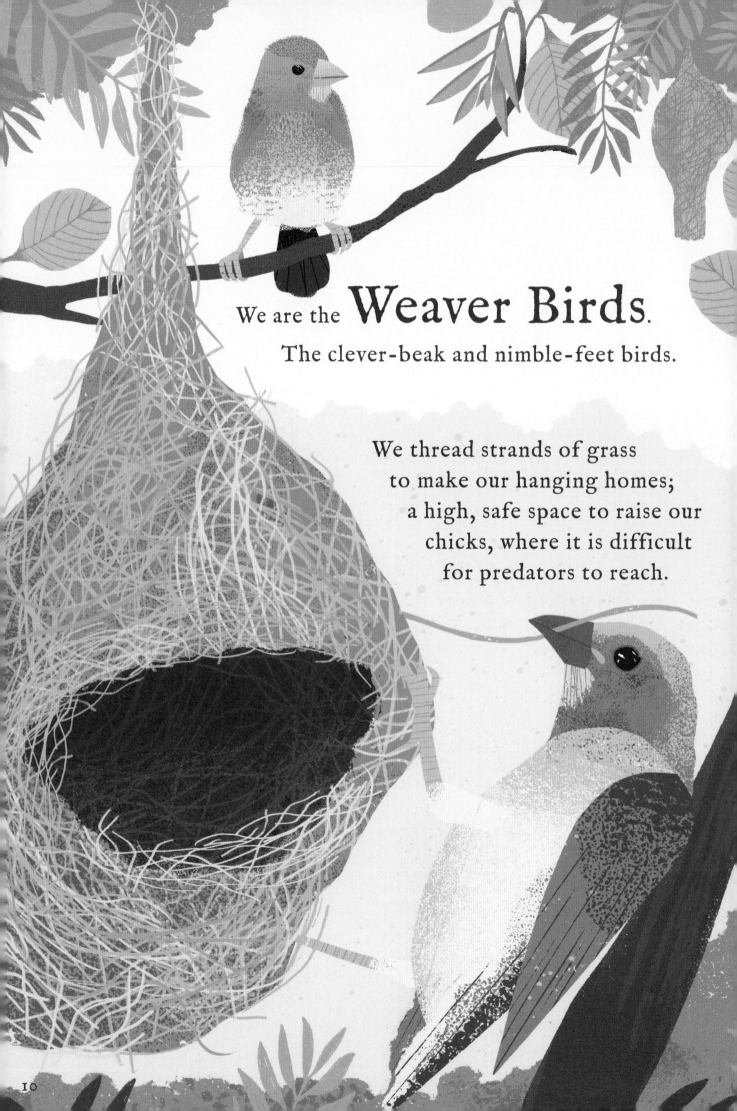

We are the Weaver Birds.

The clever-beak and nimble-feet birds.

We thread strands of grass
to make our hanging homes;
a high, safe space to raise our
chicks, where it is difficult
for predators to reach.

It is the male birds who build the nests.
Each of us wants to impress the females.

"My nest is best!"
"Come and lay your eggs here!"

Like colossal raindrops,
our nests dangle from the
branches of the thorny trees,
turning from green to brown
under the Indian sun.

We are the **Satin Bowerbirds**.
The shiny-feathered, choose-me-now birds.

We don't use our building skills to make a
home or a nest. No! We build to impress.

Our delicate bowers are built from twigs,
each made by a male to attract a mate.

Outside the bower, we lay a carpet
of beautiful blue: blue petals,
blue berries, even blue plastic.

It goes so well with our plumage,
and it will catch the eye of any
females nearby.

If the female is impressed by one of our bowers,
she'll know that the bird who made it will be
a good choice for a mate.
It might seem like a strange decision to you,
but love is a funny business!

We are the Ovenbirds.

Out of mud, we build our nest.

Each clump must be carried up into
the trees, added to the rest.

Over weeks, sometimes months,
the nest walls grow higher.
A domed roof covers the space
where we'll lay our eggs;
a curved entrance will keep
them out of sight.

We work as a pair;
we build it just right.

As the summer sun beats down, it bakes
our mud nests hard. Just like pots in a kiln.
Like biscuits in an oven.

We are the 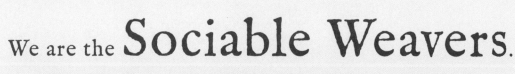Sociable Weavers.
The chirping, chattering next-door neighbors.

If you spot something that looks like a haystack
in a tree, that's our multi-story home!

Our giant nest stays cool in the hot desert day,
but keeps us warm during the chilly nights.
High up in the branches,
slithering snakes can't reach us.

Together, we've built it out of twigs and straw,
and lined the nest chambers with soft fur and cotton.

If we all help to look after it,
it could last for a hundred years.

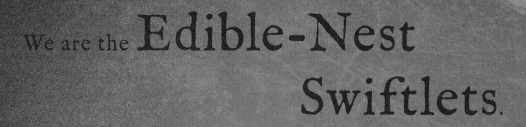

We are the Edible-Nest Swiftlets.

You might think only bats live in caves,
but we do too. In and out we flit,
catching small insects as we fly.

We build our delicate nests out
of strands of our spit, glued
to the stone like thousands
of small, shallow cups.

Each nest will hold
two tiny eggs.

We were given our name because some
humans like to put our nests in soup!

Would you like to try our saliva?

We are the Great Spotted Woodpeckers.

The canopy climbers,
the chisel-beaked tappers.

When we're nearby, the
woodlands ring with a

tap tap tap

and a tock tock tock!

Look out for us—a flash of red,
white, and black among the green.

Tree trunks don't challenge
our carpentry skills. With claws
gripping their bark, we hammer
out holes to hold our eggs.

The entrance might not look
so big, but the hole can be
as deep as your forearm!

No nest of twigs and grass for us;
just a few woodchips to line our
chicks' first home.

Hungry beaks peek out from neat
round holes, asking for food.

We bring them tasty treats;
beetles and grubs drilled
out from under bark.

We are the
White Storks.

For us, big is best.
Our nests are vast,
    thatched platforms.

Where can we build a nest that big?
We choose chimneys and roofs,
    tall trees and telephone poles.

It takes a lot of grass and sticks to
build a nest more than a yard wide!
Luckily, both parents help.

High up in our twig-twined watchtowers,
we raise our chicks. What a lofty start
in life for a long-legged bird!

We are the **Malleefowl**.
We are the mound-makers, the egg-buriers.

In winter, we male birds begin to prepare
our gigantic nest.

First we scrape a large hole, a yard deep
and more than three yards wide.

Scrit, scratch, scrit!

Now spring is coming, and there's still lots
of work to do. We scrape leaves and twigs
into the middle to make a mound.

24

Every week through the summer, the hen
will lay an egg. We cover the mound with sand.

As the leaves inside the mound rot, they give
off heat. This keeps the eggs warm, just as if
we had been sitting on them.

When each chick hatches, it digs its way out
and quickly scampers off into the bush.

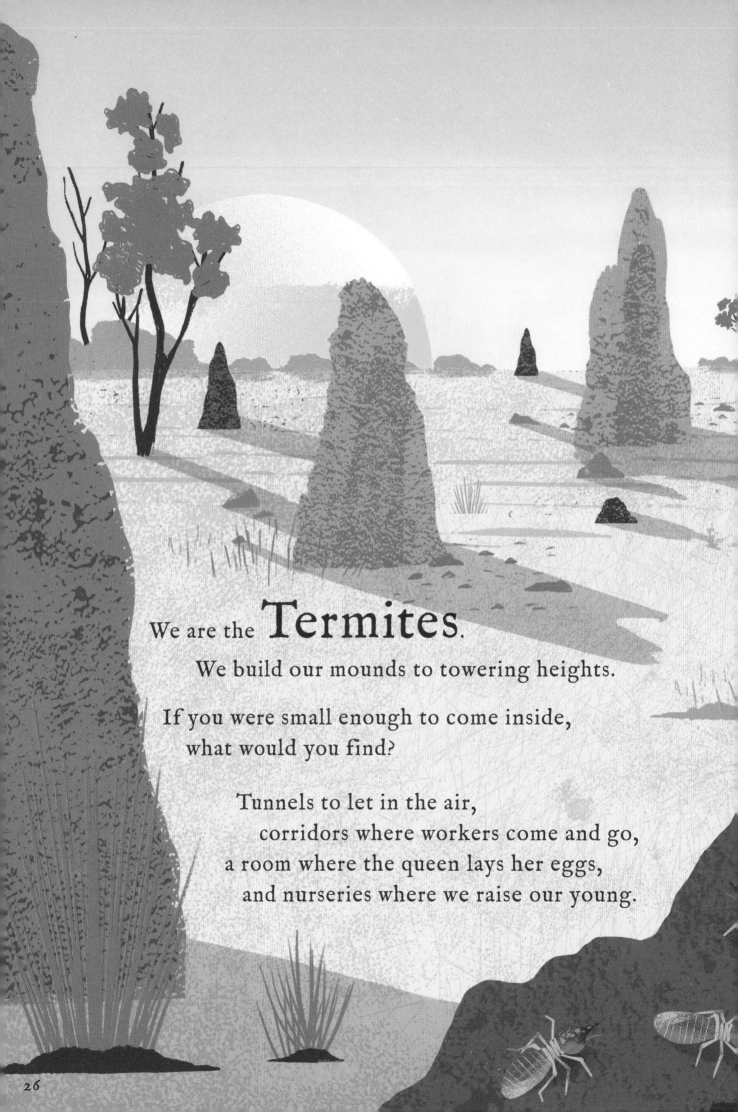

We are the Termites.

We build our mounds to towering heights.

If you were small enough to come inside,
what would you find?

Tunnels to let in the air,
corridors where workers come and go,
a room where the queen lays her eggs,
and nurseries where we raise our young.

Each hill is made of soil stuck fast with spit and poop, turned hard by the sun. Inside we stay cool, we stay in the dark.

There are millions in our colony. Though each of us is tiny, together we change the landscape.

We are the **Honeybees**.
The flower foragers, the sweet treat makers.

We collect nectar from flowers
and turn it into honey.

Our hive is our winter larder
—a store of honey to fuel us
through the cold months.

We don't collect our building materials,
we make them ourselves! Our bodies can
turn honey to wax. We chew, chew,
chew up the wax and mold
it into honeycomb.

Our six-sided honeycomb is strong,
but uses very little wax. What a
clever shape for storing honey!

Some honeybees are farmed for
their honey, but we are wild and free.
We live in the trees, we fly with the breeze,
our life really is "the bee's knees!"

We are the **Paper Wasps**.
The yellow-jacket workers.

Our nest is made of chewed-up wood,
stuck together with saliva.

Inside are hexagon cells, each one
a nursery home for a single larva.

In the spring, our queen began to build.
Soon we, her offspring, had hatched. Now
we work together to make the nest bigger.

Over the summer, the nest grows and new queens
hatch. Next year, they will begin nests of their own.

But as the cold winter arrives, there is not enough food.
It's time for us workers to die, but our nest will remain,
empty: a monument to our teamwork.

We are the **Caddisfly Larvae**.
The riverbed wanderers.

As adults, we will fly up into the air,
but for now we live a watery life, in
the sandy beds of ponds and streams.

In our tiny world, there can be
big dangers. There are plenty of
creatures that would like to eat
us for dinner!

But we caddisfly larvae have a clever way to protect ourselves—we build a little home to carry around with us.

It's a camouflaged suit of armor made of pebbles and grit, sticks and shells, bound together with silk.

With our mobile home to keep us hidden, we can even sneak up on our own dinner. It's a useful skill to be an underwater architect!

We are the **Trapdoor Spiders**.

The patient, hidden surprisers.

We don't build webs, we dig burrows.

We sit beneath a small plug of earth and silk,
hidden among moss and leaves: a trapdoor.

Out from the trap run fine threads
of silk: tripwires!

If an insect walks across these
threads, we feel their tug and...

Out we spring!

We strike!

We catch our meal, and pull
it down into our burrow.

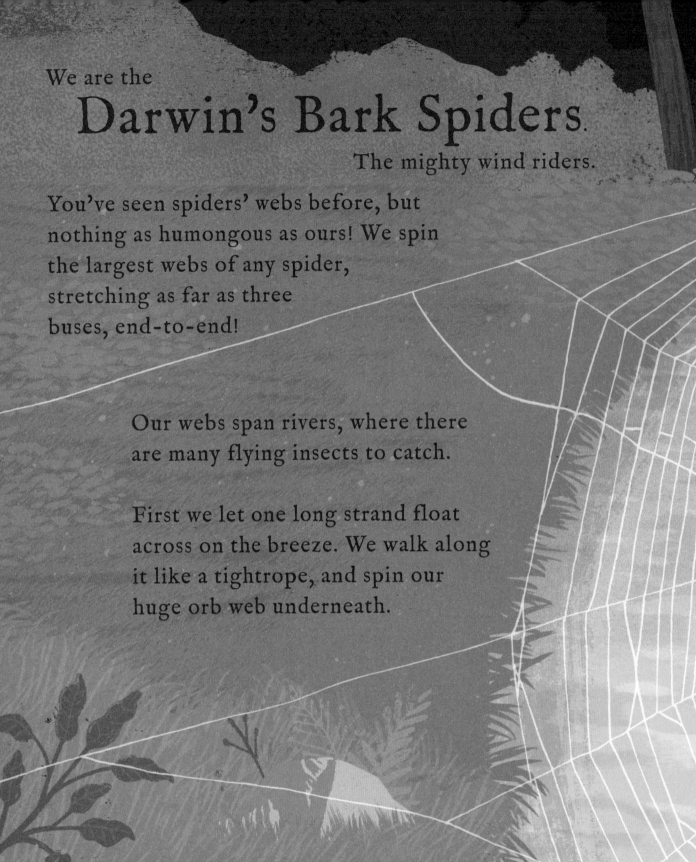

We are the
Darwin's Bark Spiders.
The mighty wind riders.

You've seen spiders' webs before, but
nothing as humongous as ours! We spin
the largest webs of any spider,
stretching as far as three
buses, end-to-end!

Our webs span rivers, where there
are many flying insects to catch.

First we let one long strand float
across on the breeze. We walk along
it like a tightrope, and spin our
huge orb web underneath.

No other spider can spin a web
out in this prime dining spot!

Such a big web needs strong silk,
and ours is a record breaker!

It's the strongest material made by
any animal or plant; twice as strong
as ordinary spider silk.

We are the **Weaver Ants**.
The stick-the-leaves-together ants.

We work as a team to fold our
home out of green, growing leaves.
Safe inside, we will lay our eggs.

Some of us pull the leaf edges
together, linking into chains.

Heave! Heave!

As the leaves are pulled close,
we hold fast. Others use larvae
silk to glue the edges together.
The strands of silk bind the gaps.

Weave! Weave!

Our colony is made of millions
of ants, so we don't have just
one leafy nest, but dozens
—a living ant town,
high up in the trees.

We are the
Gopher Tortoises.
The hard-shelled excavators.

Our front legs are covered in tough scales.
They help protect us as we dig.

When we're not foraging, we like to
spend our time safe underground.

Here, it's not too hot, not too cold.
Here we're safe from predators
and forest fires.

Though it might seem like we
don't do much but dig and eat
and snooze, we have a very
important job—so many other
animals use our tunnels.

What would they do
without us?

We are the Meerkats.
The dark-eyed desert lookouts.

We dig down through the hard-packed sand of the Kalahari. Ours is a cool, dark home below the parched desert.

Our burrows have many entrances and many chambers.

We need plenty of room because, for us, family is important. There can be as many as 50 furry members of a meerkat mob!

We don't have just one burrow—we have a dozen! Every few days we move home, foraging for food nearby. If we always stayed in one place, our dens would get too dirty.

There will always be at least one of us standing guard, stretching tall, looking out for danger.

If we spot an eagle, jackal, or hawk, we'll raise the alarm.

Buk! Buk! Buk!

In a flash, back we'll dash, into the safety of our underground home.

We are the **Moles**.
The small and velvety diggers of holes.

We tunnel along with our spade-like paws,
seeking out worms with our sensitive nose.

For most of our life we stay underground,
so we're built for digging and sniffing,
but not for running or seeing.

From the molehills you see, you might be surprised,
at how many tunnels lie below your feet.
Our network of tunnels stretches hundreds
of yards, and we're always digging more.

We even have storerooms
where we keep earthworms
to snack on later.

You see, each mole has to eat more than
half its weight in earthworms every day.
It's hard work shoveling soil!

45

We are the Aardvarks.

Our name means "earth pig."
Can you guess why?

We gouge out a burrow with our
powerful claws, digging into the
soil like spades.

Each of us has a burrow of our own.
We sleep through the day, down
where it's cool and dark.
When the baking sun sets,
out we come to snack on termites.

Though our burrows may not look
like much to you, they can be big
and have many entrance tunnels.

Many other animals use them
too. You might find a pangolin
or a porcupine in one...
perhaps even a leopard!

You see, ours are very good
burrows to borrow!

We are the **Polar Bears**.
The hidden-under-snow bears.

It is we mother bears who dig our dens,
tunneling through the snow, ice, or earth.

Soon, snow will cover up the entrance hole, and the
den will be hidden. A small vent lets in fresh air.

When midwinter comes, our
cubs will be born. Down
here, the snow keeps the
temperature steady.

Up above, the winter
sun barely rises.
The bitterly cold
winds blow.

We will stay hidden in our dens for five long months, feeding milk to our cubs, eating nothing ourselves.

When the spring sun begins to shine and our cubs are strong, we will push up and out, into the dazzling white world.

We are the **Prairie Dogs**.
The really-nothing-like-dogs.

We do live on the prairies, though: scurrying,
worrying, hurrying through holes.

"Has that coyote spotted us?"
"Quick! Hide below!"

Our burrows have many tunnels. You can spot
the entrances by the mounds of earth.

Inside our burrows we have nurseries,
sleeping chambers, and even places
where we go potty!

Though we have no tower blocks or train stations,
we do have something in common with humans:
where we live is called a town.

Hundreds of us live together, and the largest
prairie dog towns can stretch for miles around.
It's a bustling city underground!

We are the **Harvest Mice**.
The climbing-in-the-wheat mice.

With paws and teeth, we thread
and weave a nest of living grass.

Thick stems support it, high and dry,
like a tiny penthouse; hidden, safe.

Inside, our babies are
bald and blind, too new
to run or hide or climb.

But it only takes eleven days
before they're old enough
to play outside.

When we move on,
our old nests stay:
small treasures in
a field of hay.

We are the **Beavers**.

The furry tree-fellers.

With our long, hard teeth
and powerful jaws,
we gnaw, gnaw, gnaw.

But what do we build
with all those trees?
A dam that turns
a stream into a pond!

In the middle of that pond,
safe like a castle inside a moat,
we build our lodge.

To get inside,
we take a dive!

Our lodge is cozy all year round,
even when winter comes and
paints the pond with ice.

55

We are the **Chimpanzees**.
We are the apes who build nests!

It's safer up in the trees,
away from prowling leopards.
So every night, we each build
a new bed. A comfy place to
snooze the night away.

Every chimp knows which
tree makes the best nest:
the ironwood tree.

There, we weave a platform
from thin, bendy branches
and sleepy-soft leaves.

A good nest is important.
After all, we don't want
to fall out in the night!

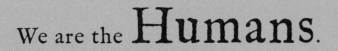

We are the **Humans**.
The land-takers, the world-shapers.

We tunnel below ground.
We build towers that scrape the sky.

We build ships to carry
us around the world, and
to take us out into space.

We come together to build small villages and vast cities.

We build out of mud, out of brick, out of steel and glass.

We may be clever builders, but we are not alone.

We must all share this world, this one planet we call home.

A Map of the World

The animals in this book come from all around the world.
Their ranges are listed in the fact file on pages 62-64.
See if you can spot some of the places they call home.

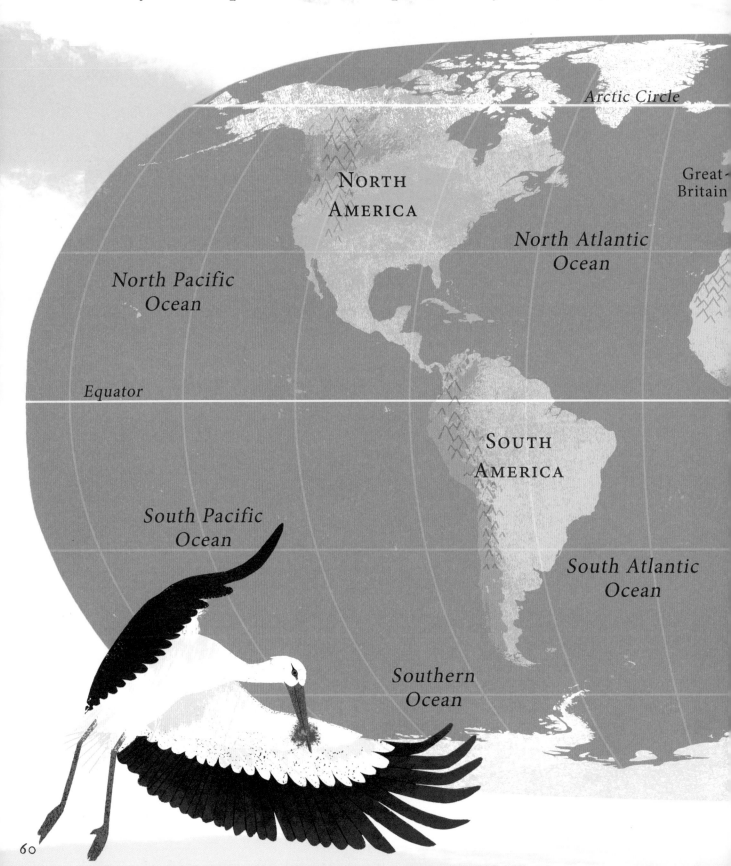

Arctic Circle

NORTH
AMERICA

Great-
Britain

North Atlantic
Ocean

North Pacific
Ocean

Equator

SOUTH
AMERICA

South Pacific
Ocean

South Atlantic
Ocean

Southern
Ocean

Arctic Ocean

EUROPE

ASIA

Japan

North Pacific
Ocean

Sahara Desert

India

AFRICA

OCEANIA

Indian Ocean

Australia

Madagascar

Southern
Ocean

ANTARCTICA

Builders' Fact File

The Bird Builders

Tailorbirds
SPECIES: Common tailorbird (*Orthotomus sutorius*)
RANGE: Asia
HABITAT: forest, scrub, farmland, and gardens
BUILDS: a nest made from a leaf

Weaver Birds
SPECIES: Baya weaver (*Ploceus philippinus*)
RANGE: India and Southeast Asia
HABITAT: hot, dry grassland and scrub
BUILDS: a hanging nest of woven grass

Satin Bowerbirds
SPECIES: Satin bowerbird (*Ptilonorhynchus violaceus*)
RANGE: Eastern Australia
HABITAT: rainforest
BUILDS: a bower of twigs to attract a mate

Ovenbirds
SPECIES: Red ovenbird or Rufous Hornero (*Furnarius rufus*)
RANGE: Eastern South America
HABITAT: savanna, scrub, and farmland
BUILDS: a nest of dried mud

Sociable Weavers
SPECIES: Sociable weaver or Common social weaver (*Philetairus socius*)
RANGE: Southern Africa
HABITAT: savanna
BUILDS: a huge communal nest

Edible-Nest Swiftlets
SPECIES: Edible-nest swiftlet or Andaman grey-rumped swiftlet (*Aerodramus fuciphagus*)
RANGE: Southeast Asia
HABITAT: coastal rock caves
BUILDS: a small nest of hardened saliva

Great Spotted Woodpeckers
SPECIES: Great spotted woodpecker (*Dendrocopos major*)
RANGE: Europe, Asia, and parts of northern Africa
HABITAT: woodland
BUILDS: a nest hole chiseled into a living or dead tree

White Storks
SPECIES: White stork (*Ciconia ciconia*)
RANGE: breeds in Europe, Northwestern Africa, and Southwestern Asia, migrates to Sub-Saharan and Southern Africa in winter
HABITAT: wetlands, meadows, farmland, and savanna
BUILDS: a very large nest of sticks

Malleefowl
SPECIES: Malleefowl (*Leipoa ocellata*)
RANGE: Southern Australia
HABITAT: mallee scrubland
BUILDS: a large nest mound of sand and leaf litter

The Minibeast Builders

Termites
SPECIES: Cathedral termite
(*Nasutitermes triodiae*)
RANGE: Northern Australia; other
species of mound-building termite live
in Africa and South America
HABITAT: open savanna woodland
BUILDS: tall earth mounds

Honeybees
SPECIES: Western honeybee or
European honeybee (*Apis mellifera*)
RANGE: Worldwide, except for the
polar regions
HABITAT: meadow, open woodland,
and gardens
BUILDS: a wax hive on a tree branch
or in a hollow tree trunk

Paper Wasps
SPECIES: European paper wasp
(*Polistes dominula*)
RANGE: Europe, North Africa, and
Asia; introduced to parts of North
and South America and Australia
HABITAT: temperate grassland
and forest
BUILDS: a nest made from wood
pulp and saliva

Caddisfly Larvae
ORDER: *Trichoptera*
RANGE: Worldwide
HABITAT: lake, river, and stream beds
BUILDS: a protective case of grit,
stones, and plant material

Trapdoor Spiders
FAMILY: *Ctenizidae*
RANGE: warm areas of North America,
South America, and Asia, Australia and
southern Africa
HABITAT: warm and tropical regions
BUILDS: a burrow with a hinged lid made
of spider silk and plant material

Darwin's Bark Spiders
SPECIES: Darwin's bark spider
(*Caerostris darwini*)
RANGE: Madagascar
HABITAT: over rivers and streams
BUILDS: a large orb web spanning
a river

Weaver Ants
SPECIES: Weaver ant or Green ant
(*Oecophylla longinoda* and *Oecophylla
smaragdina*)
RANGE: Sub-Saharan Africa, India,
Southeast Asia, and Northern Australia
HABITAT: rainforest
BUILDS: a nest made out of living leaves
stiched together with larvae silk

The Reptile Builder

Gopher Tortoises
SPECIES: Gopher tortoise
(*Gopherus polyphemus*)
RANGE: Southeastern North America
HABITAT: longleaf pine forest, scrub,
dry sandy uplands, and coastal dunes
BUILDS: a burrow up to 13 yards
long and 3 yards deep

THE MAMMAL BUILDERS

Meerkats
SPECIES: Meerkat (*Suricata suricatta*)
RANGE: Southern Africa
HABITAT: desert
BUILDS: a large family burrow containing many chambers and entrance tunnels

MOLES
SPECIES: European mole or Common mole (*Talpa europaea*)
RANGE: Great Britain and most of continental Europe
HABITAT: meadows, farmland, parks, and gardens
BUILDS: a large system of tunnels

Aardvarks
SPECIES: Aardvark (*Orycteropus afer*)
RANGE: Sub-Saharan Africa
HABITAT: savanna, grassland, forest, woodland, and thickets
BUILDS: an underground burrow

Polar Bears
SPECIES: Polar bear (*Ursus maritimus*)
RANGE: Arctic Circle and nearby areas
HABITAT: sea ice, with some returning to land during the summer
BUILDS: a den in the snow, where it gives birth and rears its young

Prairie Dogs
SPECIES: Black-tailed prairie dog (*Cynomys ludovicianus*)
RANGE: Great Plains region of North America
HABITAT: dry, open grassland
BUILDS: a large family burrow containing many chambers and entrance tunnels

Harvest Mice
SPECIES: Eurasian harvest mouse (*Micromys minutus*)
RANGE: Europe, Central Asia, and as far east as Japan
HABITAT: grassland, farmland, and wetlands
BUILDS: a small grass nest supported above the ground by grass stalks

Beavers
SPECIES: North American beaver (*Castor canadensis*)
RANGE: all of North America except Florida, Southwestern USA, Mexico, and northern tundra areas. Introduced into Patagonia in South America
HABITAT: woodland near lakes, rivers, and streams
BUILDS: a dam and lodge out of felled trees

Chimpanzees
SPECIES: Common chimpanzee (*Pan troglodytes*)
RANGE: Central and West Africa
HABITAT: forest
BUILDS: a nest or sleeping platform of folded branches

Humans
SPECIES: Human (*Homo sapiens*)
RANGE: worldwide
HABITAT: all habitats
BUILDS: a huge variety of housing, skyscrapers, tunnels, bridges, and other structures, out of many different materials